1 MONTH OF
FREE
READING

at

www.ForgottenBooks.com

By purchasing this book you are eligible for one month membership to ForgottenBooks.com, giving you unlimited access to our entire collection of over 1,000,000 titles via our web site and mobile apps.

To claim your free month visit:
www.forgottenbooks.com/free1120994

ISBN 978-0-331-41754-8
PIBN 11120994

Historic, archived document

Do not assume content reflects current
scientific knowledge, policies, or practices.

FS-179

52F
S
2

FRUIT
Situation

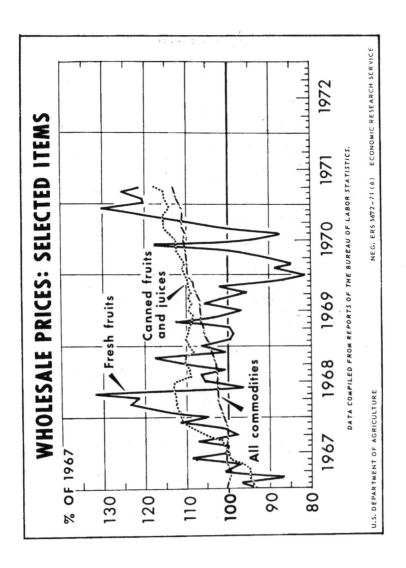

WHOLESALE PRICES: SELECTED ITEMS

% OF 1967

Fresh fruits

Canned fruits and juices

All commodities

1967 1968 1969 1970 1971 1972

U.S. DEPARTMENT OF AGRICULTURE

DATA COMPILED FROM REPORTS OF THE BUREAU OF LABOR STATISTICS.

NEG. ERS 5672-71 (6)   ECONOMIC RESEARCH SERVICE

FRUIT SITUATION

CONTENTS

Approved by
The Outlook and Situation Board
and Summary Released
June 28, 1971

Principal contributor
Ralph A. Freund, Jr.

Economic and Statistical Analysis Division

Economic Research Service

U.S. Department of Agriculture
Washington, D.C. 20250

The *Fruit Situation* is published in February, July,
September, and November.

SUMMARY

The deciduous fruit crops in the table below have a 7 percent increase in production from last year. This does not include apples, grapes, fall and winter pears, or some others. Peach production is forecast near last year's level, but the Clingstone crop in California is down 5 percent. West Coast Bartlett pear output is estimated 39 percent above last year's small crop and cherry prospects are substantially higher than a year ago. Plum and prune production in California may be down substantially from the large crops of last year but the almond crop appears 9 percent larger. The 1971 estimate for apricots is 17 percent higher than last year and for strawberries 4 percent lower.

The 1970/71 orange crop is indicated 4 percent larger than the previous season with Florida output 5 percent higher and California the same. Harvest of Florida Valencias was nearly complete by mid-June and harvest in California was still active. By the end of May, four-fifths of the U.S. crop had been harvested with fresh use down slightly and processing use up from last season. With strong consumer demand and somewhat smaller shipments, f.o.b. prices of fresh packed Florida oranges in May averaged 25 percent above a year ago and in California they averaged 35 percent higher.

The expected grapefruit crop for 1970/71 is 12 percent above the past two seasons. By June 1, harvest was nearly complete with fresh use up 4 to 5 percent and processing use up one-fifth. In May, f.o.b. prices of fresh packed Florida grapefruit averaged 15 percent above a year ago. Lemon production is forecast 8 percent greater than last season. Harvest was completed in Arizona and on June 1 about half finished in California. Both fresh and processed utilization to June 1 were below last season's levels; in May, the U.S. average f.o.b. price for fresh packed lemons was 31 percent above last season.

The canned pack of non-citrus fruits in the 1970/71 season was about one-fifth smaller than 1969/70. The carryin was one-fourth larger though, so total supply is

U.S. fruit production for selected crops: 1969,
1970, and indicated 1971

Crop	1969	1970	1971
	1,000 tons	*1,000 tons*	*1,000 tons*
Apricots	231	176	207
Cherries, sweet	127	122	137
Cherries, tart	152	119	130
Nectarines	66	66	70
Peaches	1,833	1,506	1,478
Bartlett pears (West Coast)	488	384	535
Strawberries	243	247	238
Total	3,140	2,620	2,795

only about a tenth less. The supply of canned apples is 15 percent less than last season, applesauce 6 percent less, RSP cherries 30 percent less, fruit cocktail 19 percent less, Clingstone peaches 13 percent less, and pears 12 percent less. Raisin production for 1970/71 fell 22 percent, but the saleable supply of dried prunes was up 5 percent. The pack of frozen fruits was about 8 percent less than the previous season, although the frozen strawberry pack was 13 percent larger.

About 8 percent more citrus had been processed in Florida by June 13 than the same time a year ago. Two percent more citrus remains in Florida for certified use. (Certified use excludes certain minor utilization channels.) While the carryin and pack of frozen concentrated orange juice have been greater this season than last, the movement has been about one-third more. This leaves stocks about 5 percent under a year ago. Florida cannery prices of 6-ounce cans are 16 percent higher. The pack of canned single-strength grapefruit juice this season has been about 16 percent greater than last and stocks are around 28 percent larger. F.o.b. cannery prices are 7 percent higher.

FRESH FRUIT AND NUTS

PEACHES.—The 1971 crop is forecast at 2,957 million pounds, 2 percent below last year and 19 percent below 1969. Excluding California's Clingstones, used mostly for canning, the forecast is 1 percent above last season. The 9 Southern States expect 12 percent less production than last year, while greater output will come from the North Atlantic and North Central States. The crop appears larger in most of the Western States except California where the Clingstone crop and the Freestone crop are both down 5 percent.

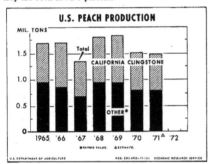

U.S. PEACH PRODUCTION

In early June, fresh peach f.o.b. prices in Fresno, Calif. were about one-fifth above a year ago while in Macon, Ga., they were around 30 percent higher.

PEARS.—With generally good weather conditions, bloom and set of West Coast Bartlett pears were heavy and production is estimated at 535,000 tons, 39 percent above last year and 10 percent above 1969. The crop promises to be of good quality. California's Bartlett crop is expected to be 35 percent larger than last year, Oregon's more than double last year's short crop, and Washington's 20 percent higher.

APPLES.—Cold storage holdings of apples at the end of May were 231 million pounds, 21 percent more than a year ago. Controlled atmosphere holdings were 63 percent of the total compared with 60 percent last year. During 1971 the average U.S. price received by farmers for fresh use has been above year-ago levels. In May it was 7.25 cents per pounds, 28 percent above a year ago. The July USDA *Crop Production* report will carry an estimate of the 1971 crop.

CHERRIES.—Total 1971 cherry production is forecast at 267,000 tons, 11 percent higher than last year with sweet cherries up 13 percent and tart up 10 percent. In the Great Lakes States sweet cherry output is 30,000 tons, 20 percent over last season and higher in all 3 producing States. Production of sweet cherries in 7 Western States is expected to be 107,400 tons, 11 percent above last year. Larger crops are expected in all Western States except Oregon. The tart cherry crop in the Great Lake States is 118,000 tons, up 8 percent. Of the 5 producing States, New York, Michigan, and Wisconsin expect larger crops. Tart cherry production in 3 Western States is forecast at 11,950 tons, 51 percent more than last year. Oregon and Colorado expect larger crops but Utah's output will be down. On April 1 stocks of canned RSP cherries were 23 percent less than a year ago and canned sweet cherries 9 percent greater. Frozen cherry stocks on May 31 were 36 percent less than a year ago.

STRAWBERRIES.—The indicated 1971 strawberry crop totals 476 million pounds, 4 percent under last year. Production in all major areas is below last year because of acreage reductions. Yields are expected to equal or exceed the levels of 1970. The California crop is indicated to be 282 million pounds, down 2-1/2 percent from last year. Fresh strawberry f.o.b. prices in California in mid-June were a little below a year. ago, with fresh movement larger. On the Eastern Shore of Maryland and Virginia, f.o.b. prices were above the year-ago levels.

U.S. strawberry imports

January-April	Fresh	Frozen
	Million pounds	*Million pounds*
1967	14.0	30.6
1968	18.9	31.5
1969	35.8	45.8
1970	40.0	55.2
1971	41.5	36.9

Imports of strawberries have been trending upward but to date in 1971 frozen are below the level of last year while fresh are slightly higher. During 1970, 75 percent of total imports of fresh strawberries and 50 percent of the frozen were imported during January-April.

PLUMS AND PRUNES.—California's plum crop, forecast at 105,000 tons, is 15 percent less than last year but 57 percent above the small 1969 crop. Harvest of early varieties was underway by June 1. California's prune crop is forecast at 185,000 tons (dried basis), 8 percent less than last year's large crop but 42 percent larger than in 1969. The crop promises to be of good size and quality.

APRICOTS.—The 1971 crop is expected to be 207,200 tons, 17 percent more than 1970 but 10 percent less than 1969. California production is estimated 18 percent above last year but Washington is 27 percent lower.

BANANAS.—During January-April, gross imports of bananas were 1,439 million pounds, 15 percent above the same period a year ago. Approximately 150 million pounds were re-exported to Canada. Average retail prices have been lower than last year. In May, the BLS retail price was 14.7 cents per pound, 13 percent below a year ago.

ALMONDS.—California's 1971 crop is forecast at 140,000 tons in-shell, 9 percent more than last year and 15 percent above 1969. The crop is developing well. Exports have been near last season's level.

ORANGES.—The 1970/71 crop is estimated at a record-high 194 million boxes, 4 percent more than last season. Florida production is expected to be 145 million boxes, 5 percent above last season. Harvest of Florida Valencias was nearly complete by mid-June. Rains during May improved tree condition and new crop prospects are good.

California's production is estimated at 39 million boxes, the same as last season but 12 percent less than in 1968/69. Navel orange harvest was completed about mid-May and Valencia harvest during June was active. The Texas orange crop is indicated at 6 million boxes, 48 percent more than last season. The Valencia harvest was nearly complete by June 1.

By the end of May, 158 million boxes of oranges had been harvested, taking 82 percent of the U.S. crop. Because of the smaller California Navel crop this season, fewer oranges have been used fresh. Processing use is up by 6.6 percent. In mid-June, more oranges than last season remained for harvest in both California and Florida.

Prices of Florida oranges increased sharply during the season, especially for oranges going into processing. During November and December 1970, on-tree returns

for processing were down to 35 to 40 cents per box, only about one-half the level of the previous season. In March the return was $1.35 per box, 8 percent above last season. Two factors contributed to the large price increase. One was the reduction in estimated crop size and juice yield caused by the freeze in late January. The other was the excellent movement of frozen concentrated orange juice during the winter months. In May 1971, Florida Valencia oranges for processing had an on-tree return of $2.10 per box, 68 percent over a year ago. F.o.b. prices of fresh packed Florida Valencias were $5.00 per box in May, a fourth above a year ago. F.o.b. prices of fresh packed California oranges have been above the year-ago price all season.

Exports of fresh citrus during the 1970/71 season have been close to last season's level.

Citrus crop—Utilization to June 1

Crop	1969-70			
	Utilization			Remaining for harvest
	Fresh	Processed	Total	
	Thousand boxes	Thousand boxes	Thousand boxes	Thousand boxes
Oranges	34,747	117,533	152,280	33,380
Grapefruit	21,251	28,785	50,036	3,874
Lemons	5,500	4,550	10,050	5,470
	1970-71			
Oranges	33,094	125,307	158,401	35,499
Grapefruit	22,232	34,780	57,012	3,388
Lemons	5,437	4,412	9,849	6,951

GRAPEFRUIT.—The expected crop is 60 million boxes, 12 percent over the past two seasons. By June 1, harvest was 94 percent complete with some fruit left in Florida and California. About 5 percent more grapefruit than last season has been used fresh but processing has taken one-fifth more. Less now remains for harvest than a year ago.

The Florida f.o.b. price of fresh packed grapefruit dropped below the year-ago price in November 1970, but by February had risen above the year-ago level. In May it was $6.86 per box, 15 percent above a year ago. The on-tree processing return of Florida grapefruit fell below the year-ago level during January and February but recovered in March. In May it was $1.98 per box, one-fourth above a year ago. The new crop in Florida is developing well.

In Texas, f.o.b. prices of fresh packed grapefruit stayed below year-ago levels until March. In May the price was $5.10 per box, a tenth above last year. The on-tree processing return stayed near the low levels of last season with some improvement in April and May.

LEMONS.—U.S. production is forecast at 17 million boxes, 8 percent more than last season. Harvest is

PROCESSED NONCTIRUS FRUIT

CANNED.—The canned pack of noncitrus fruits in the 1970/71 season was about one-fifth smaller than the 1969/70 season. The carryin was one-fourth larger though, so total supply was only about 10 percent less.

The carryin of canned apples and applesauce was sharply greater than usual but the pack was smaller. Total supply of apples is about 15 percent less than last season and of applesauce about 6 percent less. Through June 1, shipments of canned apples were 5 percent under last year's level but were slightly higher for sauce. June 1 stocks were lower for both. The BLS wholesale price for canned applesauce has been steady this season and in May was 1 percent above a year ago.

While the carryin of canned apricots was double the usual amount, the 1970/71 pack was down sharply, giving a total supply about one-tenth smaller than last season. Shipments were near the 1969/70 season and stocks on June 1 were down 30 percent. In May the BLS wholesale price fell below 1969 or 1970 levels.

The RSP cherry canned pack was sharply below last season's level and the total supply is 30 percent less. Shipments to June 1 were well under last season and stocks on June 1 were about one-fourth under a year ago. Wholesale prices on RSP cherries have been steady this season and in May the BLS price was 3 percent above a year ago. The canned sweet cherry pack and supply in the 1970/71 season were below last but shipments have been down, leaving stocks on April 1 above a year ago.

The canned pack of fruit cocktail was down 22 percent in the 1970/71 season from last and shipments were one-fifth less. Carryin stocks on June 1 were 15 percent under a year ago. Wholesale prices have been steady since the fall and in May the BLS price was 16 percent above a year ago. Shipments of canned "fruits for salad" to June 1 were below last season but "mixed fruits" were almost the same. Stocks of both were below a year ago on June 1.

The canned pack of Clingstone peaches last season was one-fifth under 1969/70 and the total supply 13 percent less. Shipments during the 1970/71 season were one-tenth less, leaving stocks on June 1 at a level 19 percent lower. Wholesale prices rose during the fall and winter but fell in the spring. In May the BLS price was 3 percent above a year ago. The Freestone peach pack was smaller last season than the previous two. On April 1 shipments were 15 percent below last season and stocks were a third less.

The 1970/71 canned pear pack was about one-fifth under the previous season but shipments to April 1 were down by the same proportion, leaving stocks nearly the same. Wholesale prices increased during the fall and winter but fell some in May to a level 11 percent above a year ago by BLS data.

The pack of canned apple juice for the 1970/71 season exceeded 14,000 cases (basis of 24/2's), 5 percent more than last season. The BLS wholesale price was steady during the winter but increased slightly in April. In May it was 1 percent over a year ago. Imports of apple juice during July-April 1970/71, set a record 20.5 million gallons, a third above the total for the season in 1969/70.

Exports of canned fruits have been mostly below last season's levels. Exports of canned pears are higher but they are down sharply for apricots, cherries, fruit cocktail, and peaches. Exports and imports of canned pineapple are higher but exports of pineapple juice are lower.

On June 24, the USDA bought 500,400 cases of canned pineapple for distribution to child nutrition programs. Cost of the purchase, f.o.b., is $2,327,350.

DRIED.—Raisin production in 1970 was 195,000 tons, 22 percent less than in 1969. At the end of May, deliveries to handlers were nearly 193,000 tons (sweatbox weight), 23 percent under the previous season. Free tonnage shipments at the end of April were only 2 percent below last season. Wholesale prices increased in the fall and in May the BLS price was 2.6 percent above a year ago. Exports have been around 6 percent below last season.

The saleable supply of dried prunes for 1970/71 was 5 percent more than last season and shipments through April 30 were 10 percent larger. Remaining stocks are 16 percent higher. Wholesale prices were reduced this spring and in May the BLS price was 2 percent under a year ago. Exports have been near the level of last season.

On May 14, the USDA bought about 203,000 cases (24, one-pound packages) of dried prunes for distribution to needy families and other eligible outlets. Cost of the purchase, f.o.b. shipping point, was about $850,000.

CRUSHED.—In California during the 1970 season, 1,506,000 tons of grapes were crushed for wine, 24 percent less than the previous season. By types, 851,000 tons of raisin grapes were crushed, 1 percent more than last season; 160,000 tons of table grapes, 62 percent less than last season; 364,000 tons of black wine grapes, 34 percent less; and 131,000 tons of white wine grapes, 17 percent less.

Average grower returns per ton for grapes crushed in California for the 1970 season were 15 percent higher than last season for raisin grapes, 47 percent higher for table grapes, 46 percent higher for black wine grapes, and 22 percent higher for white wine grapes.

FROZEN.—The pack of frozen fruits and berries in the 1970/71 season was about 8 percent less than in the previous season. The pack of frozen apples was down 18 percent, cherries down 13 percent, peaches down 11 percent, and grapes down 53 percent. The strawberry pack was 13 percent larger but the blueberry pack 42 percent smaller. Frozen stocks for most fruits on May 31 were below a year ago. The BLS wholesale price for frozen strawberries has been steady since last fall and in May was 3 percent under a year ago.

PROCESSED CITRUS FRUIT

About 8 percent more citrus has been processed in Florida by June 13 than the same time a year ago; 2 percent more citrus remains in Florida for certified use.

In Florida the harvest of Early and Midseason oranges is over. About 73.8 million boxes were processed, 13 percent more than a year ago. About 2 million fewer boxes of Valencias have been processed as last year but about the same quantity remains for certified use. In Florida 27.9 million boxes of grapefruit had been processed by June 13, 21 percent more than a year ago. About one-fourth of a million boxes remain for certified use. In Texas, processing of grapefruit was 28 percent larger this season than last and little remains for harvest. Processing of lemons in Arizona and California is slightly behind the pace of last season but more remain for harvest.

FROZEN.—Strong demand and crop damage by the January freeze have resulted in higher prices for frozen concentrated orange juice the past three months. At mid-June the f.o.b. Florida cannery price of a dozen 6-ounce cans was $1.78 compared with $1.53 a year ago. Delivered-in prices of oranges for frozen concentrate in mid-June were 60 to 65 percent above year-ago levels. The yield per box of Florida oranges going into frozen concentrate through June 12 was 1.20 gallons, compared with 1.24 gallons last year to date. While the carryin and pack of FCOJ this season have been greater than last, movement to June 12 was 81 million gallons, 31 percent more than a year ago. This left stocks on hand at 67.6 million gallons, 7 percent under a year ago. The Florida pack of frozen concentrated grapefruit juice through June 12 was 6.9 million gallons, 60 percent more than at this time last season. Movement has been about the same as a year ago, leaving stocks 65 percent larger. Exports of frozen concentrated orange juice have been about 33 percent above last season's level and exports of frozen grapefruit juice 27 percent higher.

CANNED.—Cannery grapefruit prices in Florida are slightly above year-earlier levels. At mid-June, a dozen 46-ounce cans of grapefruit juice were $4.65 f.o.b. compared with $4.35 a year ago and grapefruit sections were $7.85 compared with $7.40. The pack of single-strength grapefruit juice in Florida through June 12 was 20 million cases (24/2's), 17 percent over this time last year, while movement was only slightly larger. Stocks are 29 percent larger than a year ago. In mid-June, prices of grapefruit delivered for processing in Florida were about the same as a year ago. Yield per box for canned juice is close to last year's level. Exports of canned single-strength grapefruit juice have been 14 percent below last season.

Cannery orange juice prices in Florida at mid-June were $4.05 f.o.b. for a dozen 46-ounce cans compared with $3.30 last year. In mid-June delivered-in prices of oranges for canned juice were 40 to 45 percent above year-ago levels. The yield per box through June 12 ran 6 percent under last season. The total supply of Florida canned orange juice through June 12 was slightly less than last year and movement the same, leaving stocks at 3.8 million cases (24/2's), 10 percent less. Exports of single-strength orange juice have been 4 percent above last season.

CHILLED.—The pack of chilled orange juice through June 12 came to 100 million gallons, 7 percent more than a year ago. Packers' stocks are above last year at 34.2 million gallons. The pack of chilled grapefruit juice through June 12 totaled 10.9 million gallons, 28 percent over last year. Stocks are 2.9 million gallons, 17 percent more than a year ago.

Table 1.—Production and utilization of specified fruits, United States, crops of 1966-70

Commodity and crop year	Production[1]	Farm home use	Sold	Utilization of sales[2]					
				Fresh sales	Processed (fresh equivalent)				
					Canned	Dried	Frozen	Other[3]	Total processed
	Tons	Tons	Tons	Tons	Tons	Tons	Tons	Tons	Tons
Apples:									
1966	2,823,200	18,050	2,805,150	1,589,100	521,600	127,200	103,350	463,900	1,216,050
1967	2,697,450	16,650	2,680,800	1,567,600	553,000	79,800	128,950	351,450	1,113,200
1968	2,720,950	17,350	2,703,600	1,577,350	587,400	86,850	114,000	338,000	1,126,250
1969	3,360,900	18,250	3,342,650	1,838,500	699,150	140,100	103,800	561,100	1,504,150
1970[4]	3,174,550								
Apricots:									
1966	192,400	880	191,520	17,650	126,370	39,000	8,500	—	173,870
1967	147,525	910	146,615	10,645	106,270	22,000	7,700	—	135,970
1968	149,280	880	148,400	11,005	106,095	23,100	8,200	—	137,395
1969	230,550	930	229,620	13,870	164,450	41,800	9,500	—	215,750
1970	176,400	1,340	175,060	14,900	116,060	36,400	7,700	—	160,160
Cherries, sweet:									
1966	111,050	1,674	109,376	42,464	12,543	—	1,105	53,264	66,912
1967	110,153	1,526	108,627	40,676	14,492	—	550	52,909	67,951
1968	90,889	1,136	89,753	34,676	11,115	—	300	43,662	55,077
1969	126,800	1,432	125,368	48,228	19,160	—	200	57,780	77,140
1970	121,650	1,123	120,527	47,289	11,820	—	100	61,318	73,238
Cherries, tart:									
1966	88,966	1,065	87,901	4,997	36,738	—	46,166	—	82,904
1967	88,290	854	87,436	3,108	30,374	—	53,954	—	84,328
1968	137,404	681	136,723	4,803	48,411	—	83,509	—	131,920
1969	151,630	836	150,794	4,405	63,221	—	83,168	-	146,389
1970	118,640	682	117,958	4,980	43,358	—	69,620	—	112,978
Peaches:									
1966	1,605,000	20,650	1,584,350	598,350	914,400	22,000	44,100	5,500	986,000
1967	1,263,650	17,000	1,246,650	467,400	706,700	12,750	48,450	11,350	779,250
1968	[5]1,795,350	18,400	1,690,650	662,350	937,300	18,300	54,800	17,900	1,028,300
1969	[5]1,832,700	18,500	1,700,200	691,150	936,750	28,100	29,950	14,250	1,009,050
1970	[5]1,505,700	16,450	1,391,250	592,450	735,600	18,200	36,850	8,150	798,800
Pears									
1966	722,165	6,480	715,685	286,209	421,176	8,300	—	—	429,476
1967	451,980	4,691	447,289	186,387	259,702	1,200	—	—	260,902
1968	616,390	4,530	611,860	206,594	402,666	2,600	—	—	405,266
1969	711,650	5,065	706,585	279,166	423,219	4,200	—	—	427,419
1970	537,080	4,095	532,985	199,928	329,557	3,500	—	—	333,057
Calif. plums:									
1966	86,000	200	85,800	82,200	3,600	—	—	—	3,600
1967	95,000	200	94,800	90,200	4,600	—	—	—	4,600
1968	106,000	200	105,800	100,500	5,300	—	—	—	5,300
1969	67,000	200	66,800	63,400	3,400	—	—	—	3,400
1970	123,000	200	122,800	119,100	3,700	—	—	—	3,700
Calif. prunes:									
1966	330,000	250	329,750	—	—	329,750	—	—	329,750
1967	410,000	250	409,750	—	—	409,750	—	—	409,750
1968	382,500	250	382,250	—	—	382,250	—	—	382,250
1969	325,000	250	324,750	—	—	324,750	—	—	324,750
1970	500,000	250	499,750	—	—	499,750	—	—	499,750
Other prunes and plums:[6]									
1966	65,180	1,260	63,920	31,460	24,010	7,100	1,350	—	32,460
1967	72,972	1,190	71,782	32,153	29,829	7,400	2,400	—	39,629
1968	40,280	610	39,670	23,400	14,995	300	975	—	16,270
1969	89,500	600	88,900	38,380	40,500	7,200	2,820	—	50,520
1970	46,850	490	46,360	26,050	15,210	3,950	1,150	—	20,310

[1] Having value. [2] For all items except California plums and prunes, some quantities canned, frozen, or otherwise processed are included in other utilization categories to avoid disclosure of individual operations. [3] Apples, mostly crushed for juice, cider and vinegar; peaches, used for jams, jellies, etc.; and cherries, mostly brined. [4] Preliminary; utilization data available July 1. [5] Production includes clingstone culls and cannery diversion not sold (000 tons): 1968—86; 1969—114; 98. [6] Michigan, Idaho, Oregon, and Washington.

Commodity and crop year	Fresh sales	Processed (basis fresh equivalent)					Total sales
		Canned	Dried	Frozen	Other[3]	Total processed	
	Percent	Percent	Percent	Percent	Percent	Percent	Percent
Apples:							
1966	56.6	18.6	4.5	3.7	16.6	43.4	100.0
1967	58.5	20.6	3.0	4.8	13.1	41.5	100.0
1968	58.3	21.8	3.2	4.2	12.5	41.7	100.0
1969	55.0	20.9	4.2	3.1	16.8	45.0	100.0
1970[4]							
Apricots:							
1966	9.2	66.0	20.4	4.4	---	90.8	100.0
1967	7.3	72.5	15.0	5.2	---	92.7	100.0
1968	7.4	71.5	15.6	5.5	---	92.6	100.0
1969	6.0	71.6	18.2	4.2	---	94.0	100.0
1970	8.5	66.3	20.8	4.4	---	91.5	100.0
Cherries, sweet:							
1966	38.8	11.5	---	1.0	48.7	61.2	100.0
1967	37.4	13.4	---	.5	48.7	62.6	100.0
1968	38.6	12.4	---	.3	48.7	61.4	100.0
1969	38.5	15.3	---	.2	46.0	61.5	100.0
1970	39.2	9.8	---	.1	50.9	60.8	100.0
Cherries, tart:							
1966	5.7	41.8	---	52.5	---	94.3	100.0
1967	3.6	34.7	---	61.7	---	96.4	100.0
1968	3.5	35.4	---	61.1	---	96.5	100.0
1969	2.9	41.9	---	55.2	---	97.1	100.0
1970	4.2	36.8	---	59.0	---	95.8	100.0
Peaches:							
1966	37.8	57.7	1.4	2.8	.3	62.2	100.0
1967	37.5	56.7	1.0	3.9	.9	62.5	100.0
1968	39.2	55.4	1.1	3.2	1.1	60.8	100.0
1969	40.7	55.1	1.6	1.8	.8	59.3	100.0
1970	42.6	52.9	1.3	2.6	.6	57.4	100.0
Pears:							
1966	40.0	58.8	1.2	---	---	' 60.0	100.0
1967	41.7	58.0	.3	---	---	58.3	100.0
1968	33.8	65.8	.4	---	---	66.2	100.0
1969	39.5	59.9	.6	---	---	60.5	100.0
1970	37.5	61.8	.7	---	---	62.5	100.0
Calif. plums:							
1966	95.8	4.2	---	---	---	4.2	100.0
1967	95.1	4.9	---	---	---	4.9	100.0
1968	95.0	5.0	---	---	---	5.0	100.0
1969	94.9	5.1	---	---	---	5.1	100.0
1970	97.0	3.0	---	---	---	3.0	100.0
Calif. prunes:							
1966	---	---	100.0	---	---	100.0	100.0
1967	---	---	100.0	---	---	100.0	100.0
1968	---	---	100.0	---	---	100.0	100.0
1969	---	---	100.0	---	---	100.0	100.0
1970	---	---	100.0	---	---	100.0	100.0
Other prunes and plums:[6]							
1966.....................	49.2	37.6	11.1	2.1	---	50.8	100.0
1967	44.8	41.6	10.3	3.3	---	55.2	100.0
1968	59.0	37.8	.8	2.4	---	41.0	100.0
1969	43.2	45.5	8.1	3.2	---	56.8	100.0
1970	56.2	32.8	8.5	2.5	---	43.8	100.0

See footnotes on preceding table.

Item and season[1]	Carryin	Pack	Total supply	Shipments beginning season to April 1	April 1 stocks	Shipments, April 1- June 1	June 1 stocks	Season shipments 12 months
				1,000 equivalent cases, 24 No. 2½'s				
Total—14 items:								
1966/67	22,468	104,159	126,627	86,198	36,948	15,983	24,446	105,649
1967/68	20,989	88,232	109,221	73,751	32,498	12,454	23,016	89,533
1968/69	19,688	104,986	124,674	81,399	40,734	14,237	29,038	99,335
1969/70	25,339	113,375	138,714	87,262	48,053	13,176	38,798	103,795
1970/71[3]	31,630	91,350	122,980	75,013	44,180			
Apples:								
1966/67	1,215	3,204	4,419	2,597	1,737	473	1,349	3,648
1967/68	771	3,382	4,153	1,990	2,141	459	1,704	3,102
1968/69	1,051	3,316	4,367	1,974	2,358	474	1,919	3,129
1969/70	1,238	2,877	4,115	1,698.	2,357	421	1,996	2,698
1970/71	1,417	2,090	3,507	1,606	1,820	398	1,503	
Applesauce:								
1966/67	4,091	11,481	15,572	8,688	6,401	2,374	4,510	13,938
1967/68	1,634	13,885	15,519	7,968	7,306	2,461	5,090	13,097
1968/69	2,422	14,119	16,541	8,805	7,593	2,072	5,664	13,848
1969/70	2,693	16,758	19,451	9,256	9,535	2,782	7,413	15,281
1970/71	4,170	14,131	18,301	9,744	8,202	2,254	6,303	
Apricots:[3]								
1966/67	1,115	5,018	6,133	4,555	1,578	558	1,020	5,113
1967/68	1,020	4,213	5,233	3,783	1,450	480	970	4,263
1968/69	970	4,513	5,483	3,910	1,573	536	1,037	4,446
1969/70	1,037	5,543	6,580	3,722	2,858	453	2,405	4,175
1970/71	[4]2,067	3,766	5,833	3,569	2,264	568	1,696	4,137
Cherries, RSP:								
1966/67	102	992	1,094	997	97	42	55	1,053
1967/68	41	784	825	687	138	106	32	800
1968/69	25	1,132	1,157	921	236	89	147	1,057
1969/70	100	1,505	1,605	1,278	327	118	209	1,453
1970/71	152	978	1,130	879	251	91	160	
Cherries, sweet:								
1966/67	218	607	825	625	200	78	122	703
1967/68	122	832	954	685	269	89	180	774
1968/69	180	531	711	514	197	85	112	599
1969/70	112	947	1,059	622	437	85	352	.707
1970/71	[4]330	663	993	515	478			
Figs:								
1966/67	192	275	467	330	137	53	84	383
1967/68	84	282	366	261	105	41	64	302
1968/69	64	186	250	225	25	9	16	234
1969/70	16	334	350	208	142	26	116	234
1970/71	[4]78	370	448	198	250	33	217	231
Fruit cocktail:								
1966/67	3,440	15,781	19,221	13,322	5,899	3,223	2,676	16,545
1967/68	2,676	13,399	16,075	11,055	5,020	2,184	2,836	13,239
1968/69	2,836	16,570	19,406	13,661	5,745	2,429	3,316	16,090
1969/70	3,316	16,686	20,002	13,828	6,174	2,107	4,067	15,935
1970/71	[4]3,113	13,081	16,194	10,460	5,734	2,281	3,453	12,741

See footnotes at end of table.　　　　　　　　　　　　　　　　　　　　　　　　　—Continued

Table 3.—Canned noncitrus fruits: Canners' carryin, pack, supplies,
shipments and stocks, current season, with comparisons—continued

Item and season[1]	Carryin	Pack	Total supply	Shipments beginning season to April 1	April 1 stocks	Shipments, April 1-June 1	June 1 stocks	Season shipments 12 months
				1,000 equivalent cases, 24 No. 2½'s				
Fruits for salad:								
1966/67	285	805	1,090	617	473	137	336	754
1967/68	336	587	923	625	298	106	192	731
1968/69	192	787	979	637	342	112	230	749
1969/70	230	788	1,018	595	423	83	340	678
1970/71	[4]126	658	784	444	340	120	220	564
Mixed fruits:								
1966/67	253	535	788	436	352	62	290	498
1967/68	290	333	623	490	133	33	100	523
1968/69	100	520	620	427	193	31	162	458
1969/70	162	728	890	553	337	75	262	628
1970/71	262	548	810	558	252	94	158	652
Peaches, Calif. clingstone:								
1966/67	2,820	30,348	33,168	25,558	7,610	3,494	4,116	29,052
1967/68	4,116	22,566	26,682	21,297	5,385	2,334	3,051	23,631
1968/69	3,051	29,867	32,918	23,836	9,082	3,445	5,637	27,281
1969/70	5,637	31,479	37,116	26,594	10,522	2,194	8,328	28,788
1970/71 ....:	[4]7,458	24,878	32,336	21,161	11,175	4,412	6,763	25,573
Peaches, U.S. freestone:								
1966/67	1,774	5,846	7,620	5,071	2,549	1,033	1,516	6,104
1967/68	1,516	3,977	5,493	3,718	1,775	693	1,082	4,411
1968/69	1,082	5,988	7,070	4,138	2,932	1,033	1,899	5,171
1969/70	1,899	6,060	7,959	5,027	2,932	913	2,019	5,940
1970/71	[4]1,539	4,663	6,202	4,268	1,934			
Pears:								
1966/67	1,907	11,040	12,947	8,737	4,210	1,789	2,421	10,526
1967/68	2,421	5,756	8,177	5,851	2,326	886	1,440	6,737
1968/69	1,440	10,262	11,702	7,329	4,373	1,589	2,784	8,918
1969/70	2,784	10,590	13,374	8,383	4,991	1,534	3,457	9,917
1970/71	[4]3,190	8,610	11,800	6,834	4,966			
Pineapple:								
1966/67	4,323	16,739	21,062	13,098	5,051	2,475	5,489	15,573
1967/68	5,500	16,378	21,878	13,809	5,364	2,312	5,757	16,121
1968/69	5,757	16,464	22,221	14,158	5,700	2,199	5,864	16,357
1969/70	5,864	16,871	22,735	13,636	5,898	2,182	6,917	15,818
1970/71[3]	[4]6,811	[2]16,074	22,885	14,393	7,496			
Purple plums, U.S.:								
1966/67	733	1,488	2,221	1,567	654	192	462	1,759
1967/68	462	1,858	2,320	1,532	788	270	518	1,802
1968/69	518	731	1,249	864	385	134	251	998
1969/70	251	2,209	2,460	1,340	1,120	203	917	1,543
1970/71	917	840	1,757	1,141	616			

[1] Season beginning September 1 for apples and applesauce, July 1 for RSP cherries, and June 1 for all other items. [2] Includes pack of pineapple to May 1 only. [3] California only. [4] 1970/71 canners carryin excludes cyclamate packs.

Prepared from reports of National Canners Association, Canners League of California, and Pineapple Growers Association of Hawaii.

Table 4.—Canned fruits: Commercial pack of principal items by size of
container, United States, 1966-70

(Basis equivalent cases of 24 No. 2½ cans)

Item and season[1]	Retail sizes[2]		Institutional size No. 10		Total pack	Item and season[1]	Retail size[2]		Institutional size No. 10		Total pack
	Quantity	Percent of pack	Quantity	Percent of pack			Quantity	Percent of pack	Quantity	Percent of pack	
	1,000 cases	Percent	1,000 cases	Percent	1,000 cases		1,000 cases	Percent	1,000 cases	Percent	1,000 cases
Apples:						Fruit cocktail:					
1966/67	853	26.6	2,351	73.4	3,204	1966/67	13,431	85.1	2,350	14.9	15,781
1967/68	865	25.6	2,517	74.4	3,382	1967/68	11,677	87.1	1,722	12.9	13,399
1968/69	1,043	31.5	2,273	68.5	3,316	1968/69	14,271	86.1	2,299	13.9	16,570
1969/70	760	26.4	2,117	73.6	2,877	1969/70	13,922	83.4	2,764	16.6	16,686
1970/71—	581	27.8	1,509	72.2	[3]2,090	1970/71	10,997	84.1	2,084	15.9	13,081
Applesauce:						Fruit for salad:					
1966/67	9,334	81.3	2,147	18.7	11,481	1966/67	597	74.2	208	25.8	805
1967/68	11,078	79.8	2,807	20.2	13,885	1967/68	434	73.9	153	26.1	587
1968/69	11,542	81.7	2,577	18.3	14,119	1968/69	570	72.4	217	27.6	787
1969/70	12,728	76.0	4,030	24.0	16,758	1969/70	573	72.7	215	27.3	788
1970/71	11,160	79.0	2,971	21.0	[3]14,131	1970/71	477	72.5	181	27.5	658
Apricots:[4]						Mixed fruit:					
1966/67	3,536	70.5	1,482	29.5	5,018	1966/67	148	27.7	387	72.3	535
1967/68	2,930	69.5	1,283	30.5	4,213	1967/68	142	42.6	191	57.4	333
1968/69	3,020	66.9	1,493	33.1	4,513	1968/69	133	25.6	387	74.4	520
1969/70	3,675	66.3	1,868	33.7	5,543	1969/70	177	24.3	551	75.7	728
1970/71	2,560	68.0	1,206	32.0	3,766	1970/71	315	57.5	233	42.5	548
Cherries, R.S.P.:						Peaches, Cal. clingstone:					
1966/67	280	28.2	712	71.8	992	1966/67	24,602	81.1	5,746	18.9	30,348
1967/68	339	43.2	445	56.8	784	1967/68	17,773	78.8	4,793	21.2	22,566
1968/69	567	50.1	565	49.9	1,132	1968/69	23,049	77.2	6,818	22.8	29,867
1969/70	772	51.3	733	48.7	1,505	1969/70	24,868	79.0	6,611	21.0	31,479
1970/71	500	51.1	478	48.9	978	1970/71	19,940	80.2	4,938	19.8	24,878
Cherries, sweet:						Peaches, U.S. freestone:					
1966/67	447	73.6	160	26.4	607	1966/67	5,402	92.4	444	7.6	5,846
1967/68	564	67.8	268	32.2	832	1967/68	3,620	95.7	163	4.3	3,783
1968/69	412	77.6	119	22.4	531	1968/69	([5])	([5])	([5])	([5])	5,988
1969/70	745	78.7	202	21.3	947	1969/70	([5])	([5])	([5])	([5])	6,060
1970/71	479	72.2	184	27.8	663	1970/71	4,476	96.0	187	4.0	4,063
Cranberry sauce:						Pears:					
1966/67	3,211	89.6	372	10.4	3,583	1966/67	7,932	71.8	3,108	28.2	11,040
1967/68	3,193	90.4	340	9.6	3,533	1967/68	4,384	76.2	1,372	23.8	5,756
1968/69	3,319	88.1	449	11.9	3,768	1968/69	8,083	78.8	2,179	21.2	10,262
1969/70	3,099	88.1	420	11.9	3,519	1969/70	7,878	74.4	2,712	25.6	10,590
1970/71	3,454	89.0	427	11.0	3,881	1970/71	6,760	78.5	1,850	21.5	8,610
Pineapple:						Purple plums, U.S.:					
1966/67	11,768	70.3	4,971	29.7	16,739	1966/67	935	62.8	553	37.2	1,488
1967/68	11,799	72.0	4,579	28.0	16,378	1967/68	1,213	65.3	645	34.7	1,858
1968/69	12,076	73.3	4,388	26.7	16,464	1968/69	516	70.6	215	29.4	731
1969/70	12,396	73.5	4,475	26.5	16,871	1969/70	1,382	62.6	827	37.4	2,209
1970/71	12,311	76.6	3,763	23.4	[3]16,074	1970/71	592	70.5	248	29.5	840

[1] Season beginning September 1 for apples, applesauce and cranberry sauce, July 1 for RSP cherries, and June 1 for all other items. [2] May include some institutional sizes reported as miscellaneous. [3] Apple and applesauce packs to June 1, 1971, and pineapple pack to May 1, 1971. [4] California only. [5] Data not available.

Prepared from reports of National Canners Association, Canners League of California, and Pineapple Growers Association of Hawaii.

Table 5.—Canned pineapple juice: Canners' carryin, pack, supplies, shipments
and stocks, United States, 1966-70

Item and season[1]	Carryin	Pack	Total supply	Shipments beginning season to April 1	April 1 stocks	Shipments, April-June 1	June 1 stocks	Season shipments, 12 months
				1,000 equivalent cases, 24 No. 2's				
Pineapple juice:								
1966/67	4,419	15,034	19,453	13,371	3,622	2,123	3,959	15,494
1967/68	3,959	15,081	19,040	12,711	3,937	2,659	3,670	15,370
1968/69	3,670	13,954	17,624	13,736	2,251	1,593	2,295	15,329
1969/70	2,295	15,014	17,309	11,100	3,280	1,592	4,617	12,692
1970/71[2]	4,617	12,434	17,051	11,449	4,940			
				1,000 equivalent cases, 6 No. 10's				
Concentrated Pineapple juice:								
1966/67	613	1,526	2,139	1,224	671	190	725	1,414
1967/68	725	963	1,688	901	591	260	527	1,161
1968/69	527	1,359	1,886	1,101	428	277	508	1,378
1969/70[3]	345	1,412	1,757	(4)	444	(4)	473	1,284
1970/71[2]	473	1,454	1,927	1,092	692			

[1] Season beginning June 1. [2] Includes pack to May 1 only.
[3] Revised beginning stocks. [4] Not available temporarily.

Data from Pineapple Growers Association of Hawaii.

Table 6.—Canned fruit juices: Packs of selected items,
1970/71 and earlier seasons

Item	1966/67	1967/68	1968/69	1969/70	1970/71
	1,000 equivalent cases 24/2's				
Apple	8,889	8,726	9,365	13,390	14,118
Blended orange and grapefruit	3,738	2,187	2,578	2,419	n.a.
Grapefruit	20,991	15,826	20,535	22,124	n.a.
Orange	16,341	10,414	13,453	14,296	n.a.

N.A.-Not available temporarily.

Data from National Canners Association and Texas Canners and Freezers Association.

Table 7.—Frozen fruits: Packers' carryin, pack, supplies, disappearance, and stocks of selected items, United States, 1966-70

Item and season[1]	Carryin	Pack	Total supply	Disappear-ance to May 31[2]	Stocks, May 31	Total season disappear-ance
	Million pounds	Million pounds	Million pounds	Million pounds	Million pounds	Million pounds
Total—11 items:						
1966/67	254.0	614.9	868.9	586.7	273.8	635.0
1967/68	233.9	599.2	833.1	574.4	266.1	621.0
1968/69	212.1	676.4	888.5	577.1	316.9	633.9
1969/70	254.6	634.3	888.9	551.4	346.9	599.1
1970/71	289.8	581.2	871.0	586.4	275.1	n.a.
Apples:						
1966/67	39.9	94.3	134.2	77.0	57.2	107.1
1967/68	27.1	97.6	124.7	54.3	70.4	89.8
1968/69	34.9	117.2	152.1	59.6	92.5	100.8
1969/70	51.3	122.3	173.6	82.6	91.0	115.5
1970/71	58.1	100.4	158.5	78.7	79.8	n.a.
Apricots:						
1966/67	7.1	16.2	23.3	16.9	6.4	16.9
1967/68	6.4	13.3	19.7	15.8	3.9	15.8
1968/69	3.9	14.3	18.2	13.8	4.4	13.8
1969/70	4.4	17.3	21.7	13.6	8.1	13.6
1970/71	8.1	12.1	20.2	13.1	7.1	13.1
Cherries:						
1966/67	46.1	90.6	136.7	117.3	19.4	122.5
1967/68	14.2	101.1	115.3	98.5	16.8	102.6
1968/69	12.7	142.8	155.5	115.3	40.2	122.0
1969/70	33.5	143.0	176.5	132.0	44.5	138.1
1970/71	38.4	125.4	163.8	135.3	28.5	n.a.
Grapes:						
1966/67	8.3	6.7	15.0	8.2	6.8	9.8
1967/68	5.2	8.5	13.7	7.5	6.2	9.4
1968/69	4.3	21.5	25.8	21.3	4.5	23.5
1969/70	2.3	11.1	13.4	10.6	2.8	12.1
1970/71	1.3	5.2	6.5	3.0	3.5	n.a.
Peaches:						
1966/67	19.9	65.2	85.1	63.6	21.5	68.2
1967/68	16.9	73.4	90.3	61.2	29.1	66.1
1968/69	24.2	82.0	106.2	64.5	41.7	71.1
1969/70	35.1	53.6	88.7	57.3	31.4	60.4
1970/71	28.3	47.5	75.8	52.0	23.8	n.a.
Strawberries:						
1966/67	92.2	236.5	328.7	221.3	99.0	221.3
1967/68	107.4	213.3	320.7	239.4	88.7	239.4
1968/69	81.3	213.3	294.6	200.1	100.0	200.1
1969/70	94.5	178.7	273.2	156.5	126.1	156.5
1970/71	116.7	201.6	318.3	208.3	100.5	208.3
1971/72	110.0					

See footnotes at end of table.

—Continued

Table 7.—Frozen fruits: Packers' carryin, pack, supplies, disappearance, and
stocks of selected items, United States, 1966-70—Continued

Item and season[1]	Carryin	Pack	Total supply	Disappearance to May 31[2]	Stocks, May 31	Total season disappearance
	Million pounds	Million pounds	Million pounds	Million pounds	Million pounds	Million pounds
Blackberries:						
1966/67	13.6	25.8	39.4	22.1	17.3	23.1
1967/68	16.3	20.7	37.0	25.3	11.7	23.4
1968/69	13.6	22.4	36.0	30.1	5.9	30.3
1969/70	5.7	27.2	32.9	23.7	9.2	24.2
1970/71	8.7	29.2	37.9	27.1	10.8	n.a.
Blueberries:						
1966/67	8.2	35.4	43.6	22.4	21.2	25.6
1967/68	18.0	31.8	49.8	27.8	22.0	30.2
1968/69	19.6	27.8	47.4	30.3	17.1	33.1
1969/70	14.3	37.7	52.0	32.5	19.5	35.4
1970/71	16.6	21.8	38.4	29.4	9.0	n.a.
Boysenberries:						
1966/67	4.0	9.2	13.2	5.1	8.1	5.1
1967/68	8.1	8.4	16.5	10.1	6.4	10.1
1968/69	6.4	9.0	15.4	12.3	3.1	12.3
1969/70	3.1	9.3	12.4	8.9	3.5	8.9
1970/71	3.5	8.5	12.0	9.4	2.6	9.4
Black Raspberries:						
1966/67	4.6	3.4	8.0	5.1	2.9	5.0
1967/68	3.0	3.7	6.7	5.1	1.6	5.2
1968/69	1.5	3.0	4.5	3.0	1.5	2.3
1969/70	2.2	6.4	8.6	7.1	1.5	7.2
1970/71	1.4	4.1	5.5	3.5	2.0	n.a.
Red Raspberries:						
1966/67	10.1	31.6	41.7	27.7	14.0	30.4
1967/68	11.3	27.4	38.7	29.4	9.3	29.0
1968/69	9.7	23.1	32.8	26.8	6.0	24.6
1969/70	8.2	27.7	35.9	26.6	9.3	27.2
1970/71	8.7	25.4	34.1	26.6	7.5	n.a.

[1] Season beginning May 1 for strawberries, June 1 for apricots and boysenberries, September 1 for grapes, October 1 for apples, and July 1 for all other items. [2] Disappearance to April 30 for strawberries. n.a.—Data not available temporarily. Pack data from American Frozen Food Institute. Stocks from Statistical Reporting Service.

Item	Pack					Packers' stocks		
	Total season		October through May[1]			May 31, 1969	May 30, 1970	May 29, 1971
	1968/69	1969/70	1968/69	1969/70	1970/71			
	1,000 cases 24/2's	*1,000 cases 24/2's*	*1,000 cases 24/2's*	*1,000 cases 24/2's*	*1,000 cases 24/2's*	*1,000 cases 24/2's*	*1,000 cases 24/2's*	*1,000 cases 24/2's*
Canned:								
Grapefruit sections	3,396	3,325	3,393	3,324	3,300	1,505	1,894	1,669
Orange sections	7	19	6	18	20	7	11	17
Citrus salad	292	279	285	270	214	174	170	144
Blended orange and								
grapefruit juice ...	2,295	2,192	2,221	2,187	2,172	1,023	962	908
Grapefruit juice[2]	16,318	17,293	13,586	17,027	19,803	5,442	5,723	7,331
Orange juice	11,386	11,223	11,276	10,790	11,523	4,615	4,245	4,107
Tangerine juice	92	47	92	47	35	48	44	28
	1,000 gallons	*1,000 gallons*	*1,000 gallons*	*1,000 gallons*	*1,000 gallons*	*1,000 gallons*	*1,000 gallons*	*1,000 gallons*
Chilled:								
Orange juice[3]	88,565	100,883	70,934	84,532	90,582	21,434	30,251	32,348
Grapefruit juice[3]	6,773	7,854	6,121	7,780	10,450	2,401	2,800	3,259
Grapefruit sections ..	1,988	1,992	1,958	1,983	2,038	1,312	1,186	1,262
Orange sections	807	1,611	492	1,575	937	170	936	919
Citrus salad	5,608	4,929	5,283	4,820	4,479	2,356	2,510	2,507

[1] Through date specified in columns headed "packers' stocks." [2] Includes reconstituted juice. [3] Net pack from fresh fruit only.

Compiled from Florida Canners Association reports.

Item and season[1]	Canada	Europe				Other	Total
		United Kingdom	Common Market	Other	Total		
	1,000 bu.[2]	*1,000 bu.*[2]	*1,000 bu.*[2]	*1,000 bu.*[2]	*1,000 bu.*[2]	*1,000 bu.*[2]	*1,000 bu.*[2]
Fresh fruit:							
Apples:							
1965/66	977	1,586	591	1,468	3,645	1,217	5,839
1966/67	712	1,034	187	1,003	2,224	1,162	4,098
1967/68	669	819	56	576	1,451	808	2,928
1968/69	593	130	169	152	451	534	1,578
1969/70	830	272	39	324	635	876	2,341
Pears:							
1965/66	457	111	152	483	746	193	1,396
1966/67	502	74	38	380	492	359	1,353
1967/68	217	159	4	354	517	290	1,024
1968/69	342	2	---	157	159	234	735
1969/70	783	13	9	247	269	308	1,360
			1,000 equivalent cases 24 No. 2-1/2's				
Canned fruit:							
Peaches:							
1965/66	732	74	2,863	771	3,708	157	4,597
1966/67	852	84	2,860	1,068	4,012	203	5,067
1967/68	635	21	764	490	1,275	143	2,053
1968/69	847	4	790	595	1,389	259	2,495
1969/70	1,081	60	2,289	774	3,123	791	4,995
Fruit cocktail:							
1965/66	753	541	943	422	1,906	215	2,874
1966/67	818	843	1,040	526	2,409	281	3,508
1967/68	612	347	628	329	1,304	210	2,126
1968/69	794	321	656	444	1,421	274	2,489
1969/70	857	181	1,052	480	1,713	236	2,806
Pineapple:							
1965/66	244	95	1,367	480	1,942	72	2,258
1966/67	190	165	1,164	410	1,739	112	2,041
1967/68	201	80	876	266	1,222	53	1,476
1968/69	151	56	771	270	1,097	56	1,304
1969/70	154	88	775	305	1,168	49	1,371
Cherries:							
1965/66	15	39	646	7	692	38	745
1966/67	8	11	18	5	34	42	84
1967/68	1	8	19	6	33	41	75
1968/69	6	6	5	6	17	47	70
1969/70	5	8	287	7	302	44	351
Apricots:							
1965/66	75	8	97	37	142	18	235
1966/67	24	9	49	36	94	17	135
1967/68	17	3	14	18	35	10	62
1968/69	21	1	8	13	22	11	54
1969/70	62	1	8	15	24	8	94
Pears:							
1965/66	77	2	8	16	26	30	133
1966/67	83	1	11	18	30	51	164
1967/68	37	1	4	8	13	25	75
1968/69	38	1	9	11	21	43	102
1969/70	51	1	5	7	13	24	88

Season beginning July 1 for fresh apples, pears and canned
nerries, June 1 for other canned items. [2] Apples, 48 pounds;
ears, 50 pounds.

Table 11.—U.S. exports of selected dried fruits and almonds
by destination, 1965/66-1969/70 seasons

Item and season[1]	Canada	Europe				Other	Total
		United Kingdom	Common Market	Other	Total		
	Tons	Tons	Tons	Tons	Tons	Tons	Tons
Prunes:							
1965/66	5,814	9,229	25,641	16,029	50,899	7,037	63,750
1966/67	4,840	6,860	16,083	11,802	34,745	5,244	44,829
1967/68	4,729	6,709	14,933	11,962	33,604	6,552	44,885
1968/69	4,963	5,362	15,958	12,166	33,486	6,196	44,645
1969/70	4,619	5,719	14,670	10,647	31,036	5,042	40,697
Raisins:							
1965/66	6,662	9,591	5,115	19,382	34,088	29,841	70,591
1966/67	7,355	9,743	5,102	15,693	30,538	28,634	66,527
1967/68	6,390	11,264	5,105	16,714	33,083	29,723	69,196
1968/69	5,473	9,518	5,730	17,565	32,813	33,698	71,984
1969/70	6,099	10,340	5,279	15,090	30,709	38,179	74,987
Apricots:							
1965/66	67	2	442	646	1,090	393	1,550
1966/67	164	5	373	476	854	275	1,293
1967/68	77	5	180	209	394	142	613
1968/69	87	2	155	150	307	66	460
1969/70	105	([2])	244	249	493	95	693
Shelled almonds:							
1965/66	676	1,551	2,217	3,741	7,509	2,794	10,979
1966/67	642	1,116	1,021	2,630	4,767	3,747	9,156
1967/68	1,017	743	1,541	2,037	4,321	4,770	10,108
1968/69	1,036	510	1,193	1,531	3,234	4,006	8,276
1969/70	1,278	187	464	440	1,091	831	3,200

[1] Season beginning September 1 for prunes and raisins, August 1 for almonds, and July 1 for apricots. [2] Negligible.

Table 12.—Fruit for processing: Season average price per ton received by growers for selected fruits, by type of use, principal States, 1966-70[1]

Fruit, use and State	1966	1967	1968	1969	1970
	Dollars	Dollars	Dollars	Dollars	Dollars
Apples:[3]					
Canning and freezing:					
New York	54.40	61.50	74.70		
Pennsylvania	53.90	78.80	72.30		
Virginia	63.00	70.20	74.80		
West Virginia	62.90	73.40	74.30		
Michigan	59.50	83.00	81.80		
Washington	52.40	61.70	72.50		
California	63.80	70.00	74.00		
Drying:					
Washington	36.80	45.10	63.60		
California	56.80	66.40	62.00		
Apricots:					
Canning:					
Washington	129.00	151.00	155.00	—	—
California	86.30	132.00	152.00	121.00	70.00
Freezing:					
California	90.50	125.00	152.00	121.00	69.60
Drying:					
California (fresh basis)	176.00	200.00	249.00	185.00	167.00
Cherries, sour:					
Processing, all:					
New York	297.00	359.00	306.00	158.00	155.00
Pennsylvania	247.00	387.00	300.00	145.00	152.00
Michigan	280.00	360.00	300.00	152.00	143.00
Wisconsin	290.00	360.00	300.00	170.00	158.00
Washington	140.00	102.00	416.00	160.00	315.00
Cherries, sweet:					
Processing, all:					
New York	257.00	278.00	304.00	195.00	192.00
Michigan	265.00	290.00	335.00	205.00	189.00
Canning:					
Washington	302.00	362.00	478.00	340.00	327.00
Oregon	378.00	388.00	465.00	345.00	370.00
California	366.00	440.00	420.00	410.00	400.00

Fruit, use and State	1966	1967	1968	1969	1970
	Dollars	Dollars	Dollars	Dollars	Dollars
Cherries, sweet, (cont.):					
Brining:					
Washington	292.00	333.00	480.00	320.00	320.00
Oregon	375.00	395.00	480.00	290.00	320.00
California	324.00	383.00	260.00	275.00	280.00
Peaches, clingstone:					
Canning:					
California	68.50	83.00	76.00	74.00	81.00
Peaches, freestone:					
Canning:					
Pennsylvania	77.90	112.00	77.10	75.20	82.00
Michigan	82.00	123.00	(²)	(²)	(²)
Virginia	71.20	104.00	72.00	64.00	66.00
Georgia	55.00	72.00	70.00	68.00	66.00
Washington	67.10		119.00	—	76.40
California	50.80	73.00	77.00	57.30	48.50
Freezing:					
Pennsylvania	84.20	148.00	83.20	63.20	70.60
California	61.00	89.80	83.40	51.50	50.60
Drying:					
California (fresh basis)	65.00	70.00	111.00	87.50	87.50
Pears, Bartlett:					
Canning:					
Washington	66.00	170.00	124.00	91.00	119.00
Oregon	58.60	175.00	117.00	87.50	105.00
California	77.50	172.00	111.00	90.00	123.00
Drying:					
California (fresh basis)	131.00	220.00	138.00	125.00	143.00
Prunes and plums:					
Canning:					
Washington	82.00	76.00	116.00	54.00	108.00
Oregon	51.50	64.70	106.00	53.70	82.00
Prunes:					
Drying (fresh basis):					
California	130.00	110.00	120.00	104.00	70.60

[1] Prices are basis bulk fruit at first delivery point for all California fruits except prunes and pears for drying. Prices for California prunes and pears for drying and for fruits in other States are equivalent processing plant door returns. [2] Not published to avoid disclosing individual operations.

Data from Statistical Reporting Service.

Table 13.—Fruits, fresh: Average retail prices, selected cities, United States by months, 1966-71

Year	Jan.	Feb.	Mar.	Apr.	May	June	July	Aug.	Sept.	Oct.	Nov.	Dec.
	Cents	Cents	Cents	Cents	Cents	Cents	Cents	Cents	Cents	Cents	Cents	Cents
Apples (pound):												
1966	16.1	16.8	18.0	19.0	20.5	22.7	23.5	25.1	21.2	17.3	16.6	17.6
1967	18.1	18.5	19.2	19.9	20.6	21.9	23.7	25.3	22.5	18.4	18.4	19.2
1968	20.3	21.2	22.2	23.3	24.9	27.0	29.2	29.9	24.6	20.7	20.8	21.9
1969	23.0	23.6	24.3	24.7	25.3	27.3	28.4	28.1	25.7	19.4	18.5	19.0
1970	19.6	19.8	20.4	20.7	21.9	24.3	26.0	26.6	25.1	19.6	19.2	19.9
1971	21.0	21.7	22.5	23.5	24.1							
Bananas (pound):												
1966	13.8	15.5	15.4	16.5	16.9	17.2	15.7	16.5	15.6	16.2	14.3	15.2
1967	15.8	14.9	15.8	15.6	15.6	15.7	15.8	16.2	16.5	17.0	15.4	14.9
1968	13.4	15.2	15.5	15.7	17.3	15.7	16.1	15.8	15.9	16.2	14.7	14.6
1969	15.5	15.8	15.3	15.3	16.1	15.8	16.3	16.3	16.6	16.8	15.7	15.6
1970	15.7	16.1	17.0	16.9	16.9	17.0	15.4	15.7	15.4	16.2	14.7	13.6
1971	13.9	14.9	15.0	15.0	14.7							
Oranges (dozen):												
1966	72.3	72.1	71.9	72.5	75.7	79.0	78.6	85.3	87.2	95.1	92.0	77.1
1967	73.9	71.3	70.3	70.2	71.9	71.8	73.7	77.5	83.5	89.4	84.1	86.2
1968	89.6	91.7	93.5	90.1	92.8	90.3	94.3	103.0	109.3	111.9	106.2	86.0
1969	83.0	82.7	82.9	82.5	82.4	81.9	83.5	86.6	86.2	86.1	86.4	81.6
1970	78.7	80.6	81.2	79.2	80.1	83.6	87.8	90.5	91.9	99.0	94.5	89.7
1971	83.9	86.8	87.7	87.5	91.2							
Grapefruit (each):												
1966	12.0	13.2	13.4	13.3	14.3	16.1	16.5	18.0	18.0	19.8	13.1	12.3
1967	12.4	12.1	11.6	11.8	12.0	12.9	14.4	16.5	17.0	15.3	13.5	13.7
1968	13.8	14.0	14.2	14.9	16.6	17.2	17.5	18.5	18.7	20.4	18.1	15.0
1969	14.0	13.9	13.2	13.2	13.5	14.1	15.3	19.1	20.2	18.0	14.1	13.9
1970	14.1	14.9	14.7	14.9	15.7	18.6	21.1	20.9	20.4	18.6	14.6	13.9
1971	13.8	14.3	14.6	15.9	16.6							
Lemons (pound):												
1966	24.1	23.5	23.4	23.3	23.3	23.0	24.0	24.3	23.9	24.9	24.8	24.8
1967	25.2	24.3	24.5	24.3	24.0	23.2	23.2	23.4	24.4	25.8	26.9	26.7
1968	27.6	27.3	27.0	27.5	27.5	26.7	25.9	26.0	25.9	26.2	27.0	26.0
1969	27.0	28.3	28.2	28.3	28.1	28.5	28.6	29.5	29.5	30.8	31.3	31.8
1970	31.6	31.1	31.5	31.0	30.9	30.3	29.9	30.6	31.2	32.1	32.5	31.9
1971	31.9	32.4	32.5	32.8								
Grapes (pound):												
1966	---	---	---	---	---	---	38.6	28.1	27.8	30.7	32.9	---
1967	---	---	---	---	---	---	47.4	42.0	27.9	28.9	34.1	---
1968	---	---	---	---	---	---	50.5	37.4	29.7	31.5	37.5	---
1969	---	---	---	---	---	---	47.7	37.0	34.9	36.2	38.8	---
1970	---	---	---	---	---	---	---	46.0	38.2	42.2	44.0	---
1971	---	---	---	---	---							
Strawberries (pint):												
1966	---	---	---	43.9	39.3	42.1	---	---	---	---	---	---
1967	---	---	---	37.1	37.5	37.2	---	---	---	---	---	---
1968	---	---	---	43.1	38.1	39.5	---	---	---	---	---	---
1969	---	---	---	47.1	38.5	40.2	---	---	---	---	---	---
1970	---	---	---	---	39.9	41.5	---	---	---	---	---	---
1971	---	---	---	---	44.3							

Data from Bureau of Labor Statistics, U.S. Department of Labor.

Table 14.—Fruits, processed: Average retail prices, selected cities,
United States, by months, 1966-71

Year	Jan.	Feb.	Mar.	Apr.	May	June	July	Aug.	Sept.	Oct.	Nov.	Dec.
	Cents	Cents	Cents	Cents	Cents	Cents	Cents	Cents	Cents	Cents	Cents	Cents
CANNED FRUIT												
Peaches												
(No. 2½ can):												
1966	33.4	34.2	34.9	35.2	35.5	35.7	35.7	35.0	33.3	32.4	32.4	32.0
1967	31.8	32.0	31.7	32.0	31.7	31.9	31.7	32.0	32.1	32.4	32.8	33.4
1968	34.0	34.4	34.7	35.1	35.7	35.9	36.2	36.2	35.3	34.7	34.9	35.0
1969	34.9	34.6	34.4	34.2	34.3	34.7	34.6	34.9	34.4	34.2	33.6	33.9
1970	34.1	34.2	34.1	34.2	34.9	35.1	35.6	35.8	35.8	36.0	36.3	35.9
1971	36.2	36.4	36.4	36.8								
Fruit cocktail												
(No. 303 can):												
1966	27.7	27.7	27.5	27.4	27.2	26.8	26.7	26.7	26.5	26.3	26.1	26.0
1967	25.8	25.7	25.7	25.6	25.4	25.8	25.7	26.1	26.9	27.3	27.8	28.0
1968	28.2	28.2	28.3	28.3	28.5	28.4	28.4	28.5	28.5	28.1	28.1	28.2
1969	28.0	28.0	27.9	27.9	27.7	27.8	28.0	27.8	27.9	27.6	27.6	27.8
1970	27.5	27.4	27.5	27.8	27.8	27.8	28.2	28.3	28.6	29.2	29.4	29.6
1971	29.9	29.9	30.1	30.5	30.6							
Pears												
(No. 2½ can):												
1966	51.6	51.7	51.4	51.0	49.8	48.9	48.2	47.9	47.2	46.1	45.1	44.5
1967	44.2	43.7	43.2	43.3	43.2	44.1	44.3	45.2	46.3	47.9	50.8	52.6
1968	53.3	53.6	53.7	54.1	54.3	54.0	54.2	54.3	53.7	52.3	51.8	51.2
1969	51.3	50.9	50.9	50.6	50.4	50.4	50.2	50.3	50.1	49.8	49.4	49.2
1970	48.7	48.5	48.2	48.2	48.6	48.7	49.4	49.7	50.2	50.7	51.3	51.8
1971	52.2	52.6	52.6	52.9	52.9							
CHILLED JUICE												
Orange (quart):												
1966	42.1	41.5	41.8	42.2	42.0	42.2	42.3	42.7	43.1	43.2	42.8	40.1
1967	39.6	38.1	37.3	36.3	35.8	35.7	35.9	35.2	35.5	35.9	36.8	37.5
1968	38.6	39.3	39.7	40.4	41.2	41.3	41.7	42.3	43.5	42.8	42.8	43.1
1969	43.0	43.3	44.4	45.1	44.9	45.2	45.0	45.2	45.3	45.3	45.2	45.0
1970	44.5	44.6	44.6	44.3	44.3	44.0	44.3	44.6	44.2	44.5	44.3	43.9
1971	43.6	42.8	42.8	43.7	44.6							
FROZEN												
Conc. orange juice												
(6-oz. can):												
1966	21.1	21.1	21.8	21.9	22.3	22.9	23.0	23.2	23.1	23.1	23.2	23.2
1967	22.8	19.8	19.3	18.3	18.2	17.9	17.0	17.6	17.6	17.6	18.0	19.3
1968	19.4	19.9	20.1	20.6	21.0	21.2	21.4	21.4	21.7	22.1	22.3	22.2
1969	22.6	23.1	24.3	24.9	25.3	24.6	24.5	24.4	24.2	23.9	23.7	23.7
1970	23.5	23.5	22.8	22.5	22.5	22.5	22.3	22.4	22.3	21.9	21.8	21.6
1971	21.5	21.6	21.6	22.1	22.3							
Conc. lemonade												
(6-oz. can):												
1966	12.4	12.7	12.7	12.8	12.7	12.4	12.2	12.2	12.1	12.4	12.4	12.5
1967	12.6	12.6	12.6	12.6	12.4	12.2	12.0	11.9	12.0	12.2	12.4	12.5
1968	12.4	12.6	12.6	12.6	12.4	12.3	11.9	12.1	12.1	12.4	12.4	12.5
1969	12.4	12.5	12.5	12.6	12.7	12.6	12.4	12.7	12.8	12.8	12.9	13.0
1970	13.1	13.1	13.2	13.3	13.4	13.2	13.0	13.1	13.0	13.3	13.4	13.6
1971	13.6	13.7	13.7	13.8	13.8							

Data from Bureau of Labor Statistics, U.S. Department of Labor.

Table 15.—Apples, Yakima Valley, Washington: Monthly average prices per carton, tray pack, extra fancy, 138's and larger f.o.b. shipping point, 1969/70 and 1970/71[1]

Month	Red delicious				Golden delicious				Winesap	
	Regular storage		C.A. storage		Regular Storage		C.A. storage		Regular storage	
	1969/70	1970/71	1969/70	1970/71	1969/70	1970/71	1969/70	1970/71	1969/70	1970/71
	Dollars	Dollars	Dollars	Dollars	Dollars	Dollars	Dollars	Dollars	Dollars	Dollars
August	---	---	---	---	---	---	---	---	---	---
September .	5.31	6.00	---	---	5.23	6.04	---	---	---	---
October ...	3.92	5.51	---	---	3.99	5.49	---	---	3.85	---
November .	3.73	5.69	---	---	3.76	5.37	---	---	3.86	---
December .	3.87	5.70	---	---	3.73	5.02	---	---	3.92	5.73
January ...	3.84	5.61	---	---	3.95	4.78	---	---	3.83	5.24
February ..	3.64	5.66	---	---	3.59	4.80	---	---	3.87	5.12
March	3.56	5.91	4.91	6.85	3.70	4.86	5.00	---	3.88	5.22
April	3.66	5.08	4.83	6.75	3.84	5.10	5.16	6.02	3.80	5.38
May	3.85	5.00	5.12	6.41	4.36	5.29	6.41	6.25	3.76	5.26
June	4.05		5.71		4.62		7.55		3.85	
July	4.66		8.58		---		---		4.39	

[1] January-May 1971-preliminary.

Consumer and Marketing Service.

Table 16.—Bartlett pears: Production, 1969, 1970, and indicated 1971

State	1969	1970	1971
	Tons	Tons	Tons
Washington ...	69,700	99,800	120,000
Oregon	82,000	39,000	85,000
California	336,000	245,000	330,000
Total	487,700	383,800	535,000

Table 17.—Peaches: Production, 1969, 1970, and indicated 1971

State	1969	1970	1971
	Million pounds	*Million pounds*	*Million pounds*
9 Early States:			
North Carolina	56.0	42.0	36.0
South Carolina	338.0	270.0	250.0
Georgia	175.2	160.0	140.0
Alabama	50.0	40.0	30.0
Mississippi	17.5	16.0	15.0
Arkansas	42.0	40.0	42.0
Louisiana	7.5	6.5	7.0
Oklahoma	12.0	9.0	8.4
Texas	32.3	33.0	17.0
Total 9 States	730.5	616.5	545.4
25 Late States:			
New Hampshire	0.1	0.9	0.7
Massachusetts	2.6	4.0	4.0
Rhode Island	.7	.6	.7
Connecticut	6.3	5.4	7.0
New York	20.8	19.2	18.0
New Jersey	104.5	86.4	110.0
Pennsylvania	120.0	84.0	106.0
Ohio	28.0	17.0	28.0
Indiana	11.0	8.5	11.0
Illinois	25.2	19.5	25.0
Michigan	97.0	75.0	110.0
Missouri	21.6	20.1	21.5
Kansas	9.5	8.0	5.8
Delaware	4.0	3.0	4.0
Maryland	22.0	23.0	21.0
Virginia	44.7	42.5	42.0
West Virginia	27.4	24.0	23.0
Kentucky	16.5	12.5	16.5
Tennessee	9.4	6.8	8.2
Idaho	15.0	9.0	15.0
Colorado	32.8	20.5	23.0
Utah	15.0	13.0	13.0
Washington	4.8	40.0	34.0
Oregon	16.0	10.0	18.0
California:			
Clingstone[1]	1,800.0	1,442.0	1,366.0
Freestone	480.0	400.0	380.0
Total California	2,280.0	1,842.0	1,746.0
Total 25 States	2,934.9	2,394.9	2,411.4
United States	3,665.4	3,011.4	2,956.8

Includes culls and cannery diversions as follows: (Million pounds) 1969—228.0; 1970—196.0.

State	Tons	Tons	Tons	Tons	Tons	Tons	Tons	Tons	
New York	7,300	3,200	6,000	15,300	18,200	22,000	22,600	21,400	
Pennsylvania ...	1,100	800	1,000	11,000	8,090	7,600	12,100	8,890	
Ohio	---	---	---	800	1,000	500	800	1,000	
Michigan	21,500	21,000	23,000	106,000	79,000	80,000	127,500	100,000	1
Wisconsin	---	---	---	2,740	3,490	8,000	2,740	3,490	
5 Great Lake States									
Montana	350	1,270	2,100	---	---	---	350	1,270	
Idaho	3,200	1,600	3,000	950	500	(1)	4,150	2,100	
Colorado	650	280	300	1,760	1,010	1,350	2,410	1,290	
Utah	3,300	2,300	3,000	6,180	4,900	4,600	9,480	7,200	
Washington	23,800	25,800	31,000	700	450	(1)	24,500	26,250	
Oregon	35,000	40,000	38,000	6,200	2,000	6,000	41,200	42,000	
California	30,600	25,400	30,000	---	---	---	30,600	25,400	
7 Western States ...									
12 States .									

1 Production data discontinued.

Table 19.—Strawberries: Production by groups and States,
1969, 1970, and indicated 1971[1]

Season	1969	1970	1971
	1,000 pounds	*1,000 pounds*	*1,000 pounds*
Strawberries:			
Winter:			
Florida	16,000	14,400	13,600
Spring:			
California	268,800	289,000	282,200
Early spring:			
Louisiana	7,800	8,400	7,700
Texas.............	1,200	1,000	1,000
Group total	9,000	9,400	8,700
Mid-spring:			
Illinois	3,300	3,600	3,500
Missouri	2,100	1,900	1,800
Maryland	2,200	1,900	1,900
Virginia	3,500	3,300	2,600
North Carolina	3,900	3,600	3,800
Kentucky	2,900	2,600	2,400
Tennessee	3,000	2,400	3,200
Arkansas	6,100	4,200	3,500
Oklahoma	4,300	1,700	1,900
Group total	31,300	25,200	24,600
Late spring:			
Massachusetts	1,200	1,200	1,200
New York	5,400	6,300	5,800
New Jersey	7,900	6,800	7,700
Pennsylvania	4,600	4,800	5,000
Ohio	4,300	4,000	3,600
Indiana	2,600	2,600	3,100
Michigan	33,400	25,400	24,600
Wisconsin	5,200	4,900	4,800
Washington	26,100	29,900	28,000
Oregon	69,900	70,800	63,600
Group total	160,600	156,700	147,400
All States	485,700	494,700	476,500

[1] Includes processing.

Table 20.—Citrus fruits: Production, 1968/69, 1969/70, and indicated 1970/71[1]

Crop and State	1968/69	1969/70	1970/71
	1,000 boxes[2]	1,000 boxes[2]	1,000 boxes[2]
Oranges:			
Early, Midseason and Navel varieties:[3]			
California	18,600	21,200	18,000
Florida	69,700	72,900	82,200
Texas	2,800	2,800	4,000
Arizona	1,270	1,120	900
Total	92,370	98,020	105,100
Valencias:			
California	25,700	17,800	21,000
Florida	60,000	64,800	63,000
Texas	1,700	1,400	2,200
Arizona	4,110	3,640	2,600
Total	91,510	87,640	88,800
All oranges:			
California	44,300	39,000	39,000
Florida	129,700	137,700	145,200
Texas	4,500	4,200	6,200
Arizona	5,380	4,760	3,500
Total oranges	183,880	185,660	193,900
Grapefruit:			
Florida, all	39,900	37,400	43,000
Seedless	27,700	27,900	31,200
Pink	10,700	10,200	10,900
White	17,000	17,700	20,300
Other	12,200	9,500	11,800
Texas	6,700	8,100	10,100
Arizona	2,510	3,160	2,500
California, all	5,060	5,250	4,800
Desert Valleys	3,260	2,950	2,700
Other areas	1,800	2,300	2,100
Total Grapefruit	54,170	53,910	60,400
Lemons:			
California	12,300	12,700	13,500
Arizona	3,510	2,820	3,300
Total lemons	15,810	15,520	16,800
Limes:			
Florida	700	725	880
Tangeloes:			
Florida	1,800	2,500	2,700
Tangelos:			
Florida	3,400	3,000	3,700
Arizona	170	220	200
California	640	760	800
Total tangerines	4,210	3,980	4,700
Temples:			
Florida	4,500	5,200	5,000

[1] The crop year begins with the bloom of the first year shown and ends with completion of harvest of the following year. [2] Net content of box varies. Approximate averages are as follows: Oranges - California and Arizona, 75 lbs.; other States, 90 lbs.; Grapefruit - California, Desert Valleys, and Arizona, 64 lbs.; other California area, 67 lbs.; Florida, 85 lbs. and Texas, 80 lbs.; Lemons - 76 lbs.; Limes - 80 lbs.; Tangelos - 90 lbs.; Tangerines - California and Arizona, 75 lbs.; Florida, 95 lbs.; and Temples - 90 lbs. [3] Navel and Miscellaneous varieties in California and Arizona. Early and Midseason varieties in Florida and Texas, including small quantities of tangerines in Texas.

LIST OF TABLES

TFS-179   **JULY 1971**

Lightning Source UK Ltd.
Milton Keynes UK
UKHW051332080219
336748UK00033B/1366/P